Seven Stars More!

Kathy Mallat

WALKER AND COMPANY NEW YORK

Abby isn't tired . . .

so she counts the sheep nearby.

"1 , 2 , 3 , 4,

5 , 6 , 7 , more."

Then she counts her fish ,
flying way up high.

"1 🐟, 2 🐟, 3 🐟, 4,

5 🐟, 6 🐟, 7 🐟, more."

Abby counts the dots
on both of her bears.

"1 ⬤ , 2 ⬤ , 3 ⬤ , 4,

5 ⬤ , 6 ⬤ , 7 ⬤ , more."

She counts the stripes
on the shirt that she wears.

"1 ▬ , 2 ▬ , 3 ▬ , 4,

5 ▬ , 6 ▬ , 7 ▬ , more."

Abby counts the books
that she has just read.

"1 , 2 , 3 , 4,

5 , 6 , 7 , more."

She counts her leaves
scattered next to the bed.

"1 , 2 , 3 , 4,
5 , 6 , 7 , more."

She counts her puppets
as they dance and spin.

"1 , 2 , 3 , 4,

5 , 6 , 7 , more."

Then Abby counts her toes,
and tucks them in.

"1 , 2 , 3 , 4,

5 , 6 , 7 , more."

At last, as she tries
counting stars on her bed,

"1 ★ , 2 ★ , 3 ★ , 4,

Abby snuggles in and falls asleep instead.

5 ★ , 6 ★ , 7 ★ . . .

snore."

For Mom

With special thanks to
Britany Sewell
and
Mariah Easton

First published in the United States of America in 1998 by Walker Publishing Company, Inc.
Published simultaneously in Canada by Thomas Allen & Son Canada, Limited, Markham, Ontario

Library of Congress Cataloging-in-Publication Data
Mallat, Kathy.
Seven stars more!/Kathy Mallat
p.   cm
Summary: When Abby isn't tired at bedtime, she counts sheep and almost everything else in her bedroom.
ISBN 0-8027-8675-8. —ISBN 0-8027-8676-6 (reinforced)
[1. Sleep—Fiction. 2. Bedtime—Fiction. 3. Counting]
I. Title.
PZ7.M29455Se   1998
[E]—dc21   98–6497
                                 CIP
                                 AC

Book design by Sophie Ye Chin

Printed in Hong Kong
2 4 6 8 10 9 7 5 3 1